STiLL HUMAN

ISBN 978-1-953868-02-2

Book cover design by Audrey Mei at Falkenberg Press.
Detail from Hieronymus Bosch, *The Garden of Earthly Delights*.
Museo del Prado, Madrid.

First edition 2025.

Falkenberg Press
Berkeley, California 94709
www.falkenbergpress.com

www.keithgaboury.com

TABLE OF CONTENTS

II.

III.

IV.

I WOKE UP

in a root of speed
where tree ring limbs
sprouted through my boyhood's
bed frame confinement.
The door opened to you
spotting my boysenberries
bursting within a box
of adolescent air.
       Oh My
dropped from your lips
like construction bricks.

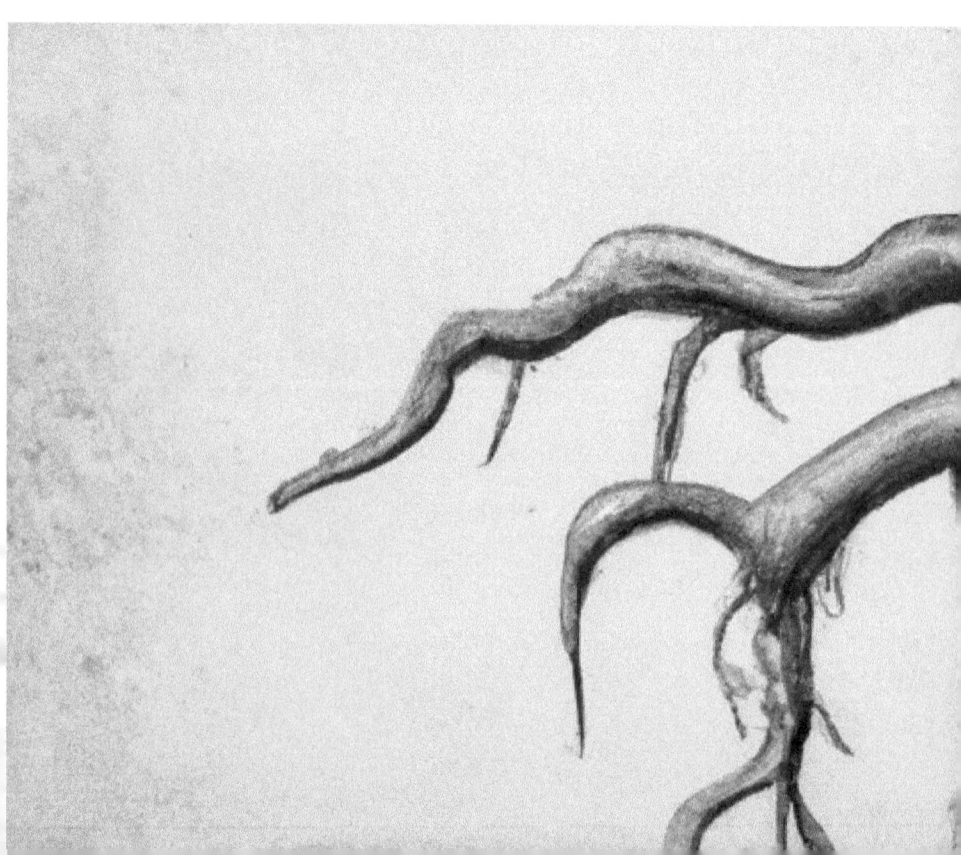

I of course draped
nature's exposure
under my blue-earth blanket.
Can we devour this memory
like inhaling a maple branch?
Father's Sunday pancakes
muscled out a breakfast welcome
under the bathroom frame
where my juice
squirmed down
our hungry drain.

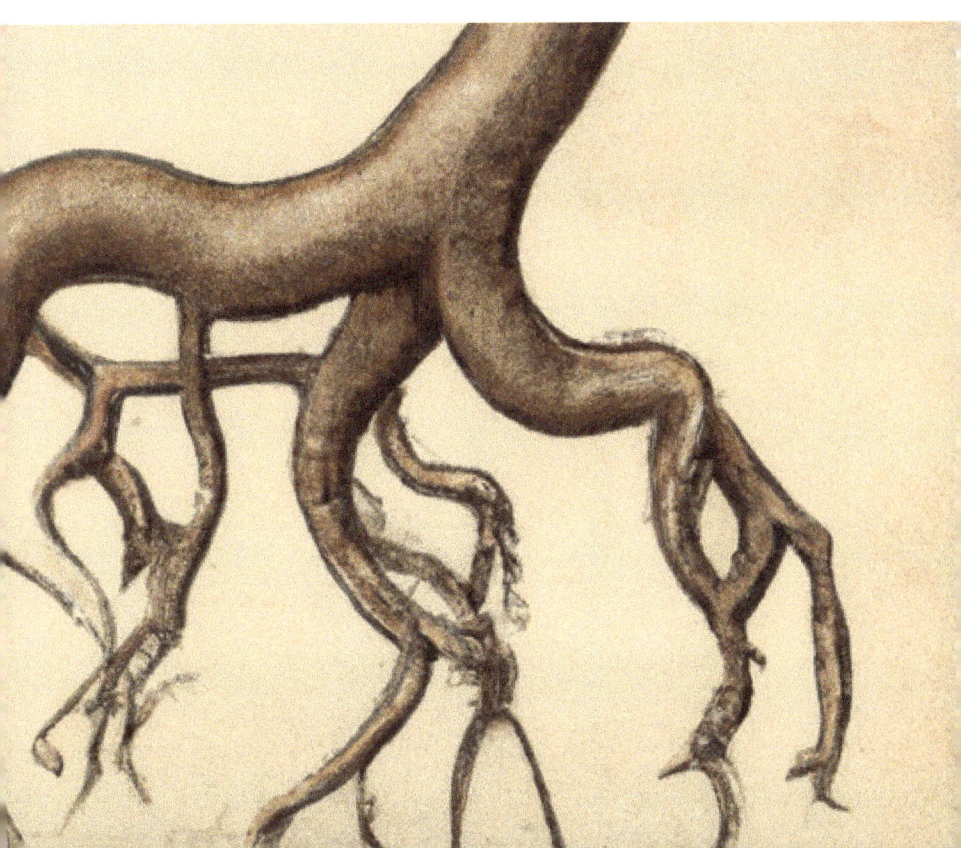

RUBBER MAGIC

You snuck into Ma's bedroom / to grab some lipstick for your
preschool lips / when you found her dildo poking its head /
out of the top drawer like a prairie dog / But you would have
never called Ma a dog as you clutched the shaft / Curiosity I
suppose for the black phallic laying bare /

Before the enchantment of your eyes / you picked up your
wand and yelled *Abracadabra* / to my head poking in / I
slapped the rubber away / yet I couldn't clean your hand
from rubbed-on spells never told

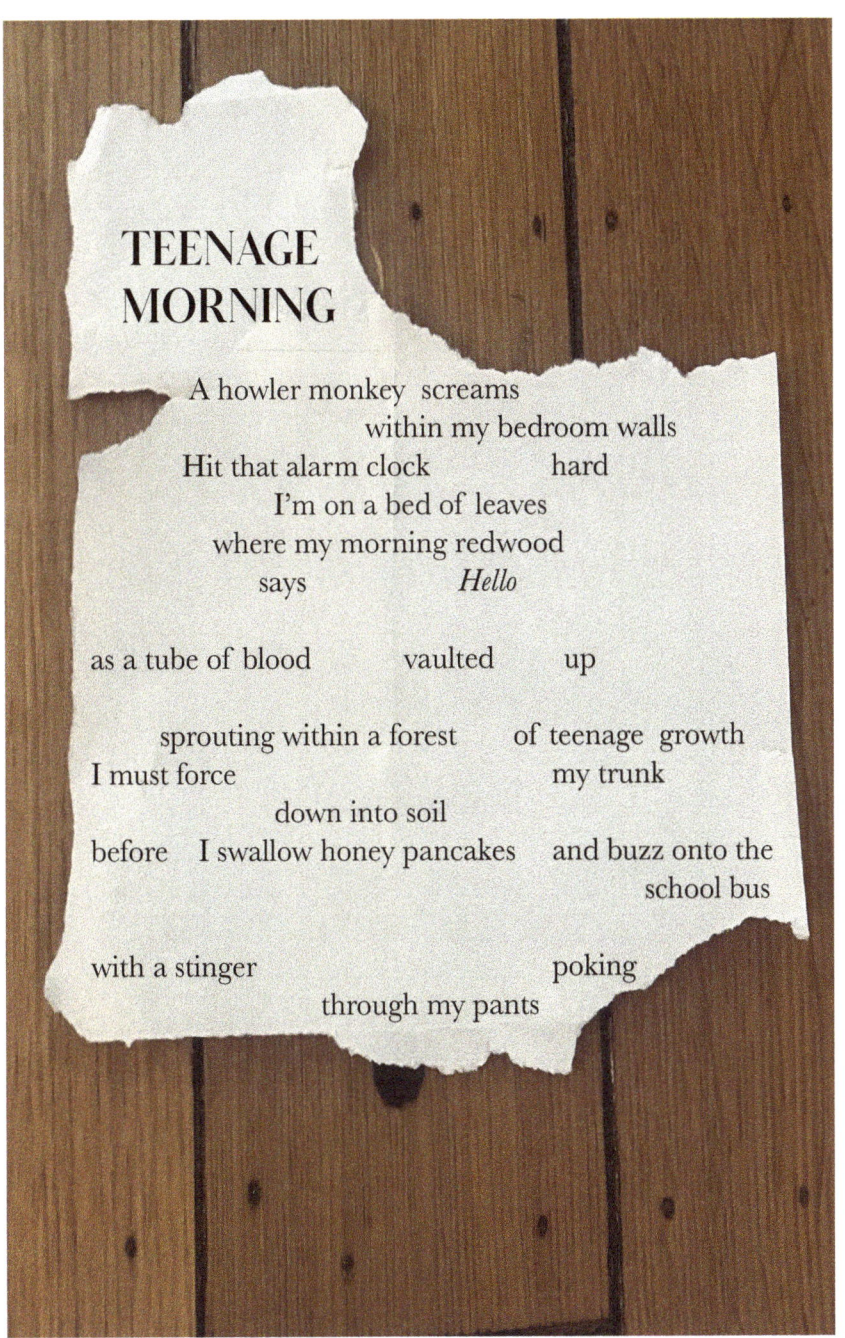

TEENAGE
MORNING

A howler monkey screams
within my bedroom walls
Hit that alarm clock   hard
I'm on a bed of leaves
where my morning redwood
says   *Hello*

as a tube of blood   vaulted   up

sprouting within a forest   of teenage growth
I must force   my trunk
down into soil
before   I swallow honey pancakes   and buzz onto the
school bus

with a stinger   poking
through my pants

TEENAGE MORNING II

You snuck into Ma's bedroom

where her   red lipstick

vaulted up like a prairie dog

You clutched the shaft

of teenage growth

Before the enchantment of your eyes

I slapped the red  away

Then we swallowed pancakes

and buzzed to the honey school bus

YOU
SHOULD
BE
FATTER

Mom tells me. I try
to shrug her off like a snail
I can't pry from my stomach.

In the bathroom, an air freshener
sprays that snail

while the mirror keeps on
throwing my reflection back.

Over a porcelain circle,
I force my finger down.

Breakfast rushes out
like swamp water
hosting mollusks of disgust.

STONE BABY

*"A fetus dies during an abdominal pregnancy,
is too large to be reabsorbed by the body, and calcifies."*

You carry me,   a reject
                                          of black stone
              silently   screaming
         beside my   sister

<hr>

              still   alive
         when you   penetrate
the clinic's sliding door   sword

         After you open   your legs
for a sterilized   invasion
                   on an amniotic battlefield

<hr>

will you   remember
                   your twin daughters

         preserved in the cellular   thumbprint
pressed into your prom   dress belly
         In utero   bold cells   expanded
into my emerging   brain

<hr>

              Now I'm calcified
              within a canopy
              of skin and bone

16

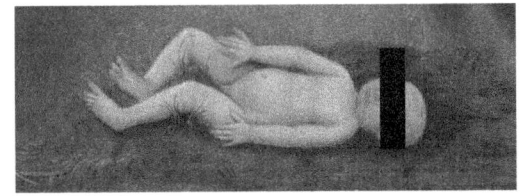

THE RADIOACTIVE HORSE

His hooves plowed through
your shut closet. In your bedroom,
you got weighed down

in a hailstorm of uranium.
An aquitaine occupation,

the horse neighed a bucking desire
to call your womb, your egg mistake
his territorial property.

When you stepped over to calm
his haunch, he snorted a punch
like Pa's fist across Ma's jaw.

This spawn burned scars
into your fallopian hallways.

You felt a pulse reverberating.
The ultrasound revealed
a hole in my spiked heart.

HIBISCUS IN OUR BEDROOM

My dick split open
into a blooming hibiscus
on the matrimony mattress
we've stopped claiming
in the union of us.

Your sleeping chest
       heaved   up   and   down
while five newborn petals
extended themselves anew.

My manhood never won
a gold medal in swimming
backflips of fertilization.
Would my flower be victorious?

Doorbell chimed, I sprang up
to greet a honeybee
voracious for the nectar I secreted.

When you awoke to a hairy body
latched onto my pink creation,
rage pollinated your face
against the bee's stinger
waving a satisfied goodbye.

I could only offer my hibiscus
dripping paternal-spiked nectar
under our bedroom glare.

10:40 AM

WITH

DR. SAMSON

Please drop your trousers.

My trousers? Oh right.
Jeans met Jordans,

I swallowed spit
in between an eternity of coughing

and her rubber hands squeezing
what made a Berkeley nurse proclaim

It's A Boy! a quarter century before.

Once I pulled up my torn jeans
and muttered some prepackaged questions

about her due date
and the baby shower to come,

Dr. Samson sat down
twenty-six weeks into full term.

Her meconium-green eyes
swiveled before mine:

You can still be a father.

A LOG PARABLE

My Grandma once told me a log family found security along a riverbank while a wolf disemboweled a man around the bent neck of an ephemeral flow. The man screamed horror, his organs splayed out under a wraparound-hug moon,

but the family didn't hear his pain. Sprung from the expanse of his wet bark tongue, the Pa recited *The Little Red Riding Hood* to his daughter. Over a winter's waxing and waning bedtimes, the tale wiggled itself like a hookworm into her consciousness. With her brain heavy with parasitic words of forested danger, she rolled herself to lay within the thumbprint of waning winter moonlight.

Heart tendrils on his lips, the wolf growled towards the family. The Ma and Pa whispered as one to their only kin *he will not eat you, he will not eat you.* Over the daughter, he stopped

where blood dripped onto her girlhood. As water shoved the stain away, the wolf hunted on into a night's open mouth.

RUNAWAY LEGS

In his Manhattan bed, Pablo shrieks
    over street   honking.

Belly-flopping
        down, he finds
    his after-dinner smoke

beside a turkey thigh
taunting his   subtraction.
How cruel he mutters to Sally.

Sally purrs with laughter
as Pablo duck tapes his hands

to vault his torso   up,
plop onto the windowsill
like a bear   up a redwood.

There he gawks at his   legs:
        they run through
a Houston   intersection,

stop before a dirty
bodega's doorway,

gape inside with phantom sight
upon a deli spread

beckoning an invitation
of distrustful ingestion.

Pablo squints at the surreal
        (could he identify his legs
                in a leg line-up?)

when he slips, bruising his
        paper skin
on the hardwood floor.

HEARTLESS

Neighbors and strangers
gawked at the pothole
in the left avenue of my chest.

I just shrugged, mumbled something
about a better self I'm working on.

O positive blood sputtered out
as I slid past Central Park's
unhoused sight

to my girlfriend Hazel
who stood before the Alice
in Wonderland statue.

With an absence
of future anniversary glee,
I had negative desire

to kiss her symmetrical face
when those Big Apple eyes

gaped into my hole
as if she got transfixed
before a foreign ocean.

This went on
equal to the bite of time needed
to swallow a banana.

I could be a husband-in-waiting
or a sideshow for only so long
so I broke up with her

like defenestrating a banana peel
into a NYC afternoon.

Under an unshackled sun,
I rang my Ma on one-percent battery.

> *Son, your heart chambers*
> *are my greatest gift to you.*

Back to my apartment building
with a dead phone,

I saw my heart, flattened by feet
on a Tompkins Square sidewalk,

sheltering years of beats
not yet lived.

ANIMAL SWITCH

David broke his new year's day leg
on a Goodland, Kansas, riverbank.
After a snail took the afternoon   to slime down,
she braced his limb
into a fusion of movement

                              up up through the mud
to Jack & Dick's Pawn Shop
where he bartered his splintered femur

for an Animal Switch
glued over his beard's black roots.
With one   foot sinking
into a wet cement clasp, he jolted
into a thoroughbred-constructed body

                              we call Charlie.

Out in the prairie of wayward grandfathers,
Charlie sprouted a black moon tail
and Delta brown fur. Once his haunch
            found full bloom, a pound of happiness
plopped onto his back

Yet some cornstalk   f amily
led by the chromosomal twist of

                              Fucken Fred

who tossed out a wet Charlie
when his neighs
showered with the daughter's lathered DNA.

Once he stomped Fred's head
like a pumpkin in   decomposition,
Charlie trotted up the stpes
to a house his brain told him
he belonged. As his hooves   landed
on that manufactured

                              Welcome Home mat,
Juno leveled in her corporate suit
I wanna make   a baby tonight.

Can a horse   perform on command?
Charlie galloped to his bedroom's

                              screaming red walls
      to rip that switch away.
A wildfire of blood
lashed into the carpet's   understory

                              where David collapsed
his weight in homonid sleep.

YOU'RE GUILTY
OF BEING A WOMAN

when you drag the womb
of your womanhood

down the Gratification Aisle.
You pick a price-slashed clitoris

since the one Ma gave you
got kicked in the shin

after you and David failed
to fuck a baby into reality
through those hot pandemic months of 2020.

Does that make you a failed slut?

You ought to host a slut conference
so experts finally define
who falls in / who falls out.

Your purchase slaps
onto the checkout counter.

A male employee
stares back

as if he ravishes
to cage all your unmarried orgasms.

Does this make you a confined slut?

Home unlocked,
you slip your pleasure into place

when the bank calls:
Your account is terminated.

We don't support sluts
in the twenty-first century.

PAST LIFE RECONSTRUCTED

I am a man though I believe
I once breathed as a mother
in low sunlight who drank milk
from cows grazed in cemeteries.

Under the same moon
I blink under now, she nursed
her neonate son before a fire's

dancing limbs. I wonder
about the trajectory of mortal flesh
seeped into grass, ruminated
in cow stomachs, then filled her own,

sending a calcium cocktail
from her breast to the son
enveloped in her grasp.

The moonlit man I am
digs through veneers of deaths and births
to hold this mother's skin
alive in my neurological hands.

II

BASED ON A TRUE STORY

Back in the beginning, Eve snatched an apple from a branch and tore her teeth into that red sphere. Yet when Adam swallowed the southern hemisphere,

a chunk happily lodged itself next to his larynx. She peered down to the apple yelling *fuck you* — the first *fuck* ejected in the history of human-to-apple relations.

An arm around her shoulders, Adam leaned into Eve as they quickened their heartbeats to the neighborhood hospital run by esteemed squirrels and rabbits. With his brain searching for oxygen like a roofless man searching for a bed, Adam shoved in a free-of-charge twig. The apple chunk screamed. He kept on jabbing until he wheezed out words to a beaver mother whose son's tail got ripped off by a bear.

Up at the timber desk, Eve pleaded with a squirrel receptionist who consumed his gaze on stashing lunch acorns away. So she slapped down a Customer Dissatisfaction Survey onto the employee's tongue smeared with sap.

Between waiting room logs, Adam collapsed, his blue-sky face gaping up at apathetic clouds. His body flung over the desk by a heave of estrogen strength, they cracked the solitude of Dr. Furry Rabbit who lit his rolled smoke in an ascending dusk.

Hey are you the new bipeds everyone's talking about?
Yes and this apple won't let Adam breathe.
Well have you tried my fire?

A match flicked inside scorched his heart black. After she spat out that destruction, Eve thought of her two hearts born flush from the Earth. Once she paid a quarter lung co-pay, Dr. Furry Rabbit stitched-up the transplant with threads plucked from his fur.

Snug in the circle of waxing moonlight, Adam pressed his palm over his female pulse.

They shambled back toward the soil of our genesis, but they couldn't enter the garden. Its gate was locked; the tree's ripeness burned to the ground.

CONFESSION

I slip into the ██████████████████████ sin box
after I lied to my dentist
through   bleeding   gums
about my flossing regiment

Inside His   ████████████   judgment
a spike of light   crawls into my   eyes
like a rat looking for a   home

Why am I infested with ████████████ *vice*
I either think but   do not
speak or   speak
but do not   think

Thinking   and   Speaking
got   divorced   last December
They got   sequestered
at opposite ██████████████████ ends of my skull

In San Francisco heat ██████████ who am I ██████████
I do not have   a job
to say hello   and   goodbye
so I kick   a pigeon   at 16th and ██Church██

The Father said my   forgiveness
is a breakfast plate
to consume   ████████ raw ████████
under an   egg   sun

41

CONFESSION REDACTED

I slip into ██████████████████████ █████
██████████████ my dentist
██████ bleeding ██████
██████████████████

Inside His ██████████ ██████
██ spike of light   eyes
like a rat looking for ██ ██████

██████████ ██████████████████
██████████ ██████
██████████ ██████
██████ ██████

    Thinking   and   Speaking
██ ██████████
██████████████
at opposite ████████████████████ ends of ██████
              sequestered

██ San Francisco heat ██████████ who am I ██████
  I ██████ have ██████
         to ██████ ██████
██ kick   a pigeon ██████ and ██████

The Father ██████ ██████
██████████████████
██████ raw ██████
██████ sun

I LEFT MY NORTH OAKLAND SHADOW

In the oxygen bath
of Ocean Beach, a wind's swirling arms
shoved me back onto my ass

Under a crushed seashell,
my heart slunk out across sand.
She slimed away

                                     towards a rose garden
                          before the Dutch Windmill's
                               swirling petal blades.

I sprinted inland
to grab a hunk of Alamo Square grass
Roots in hand,

I flipped my finger at the native glory
of the Painted Ladies' sheen.

Did I scandalize
the four postcard temples?
A fanny pack tourist chuckled,

his money legs jogging over
for a selfie with my heartless frame
but I pushed him into a gutter.

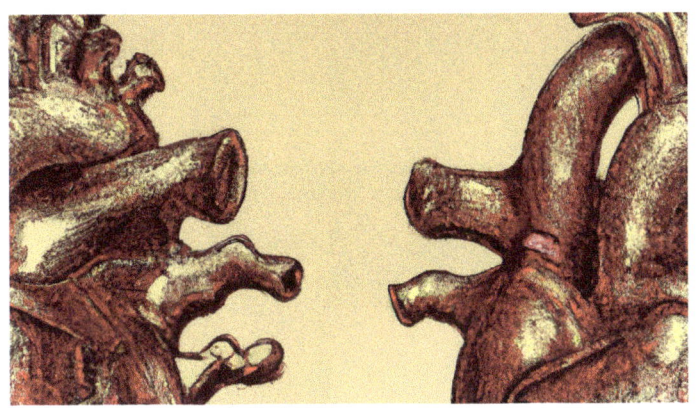

I needed to find my red friend
lost within a grid
I couldn't grapple.

Into a neighborhood I once lived
and now despise, I found her

sobbing on a Panhandle sidewalk,
a broken petal on her lips,
she exclaimed
I saved some nectar for you.

I smiled and stuffed her
behind my ribs: she snuggled oh so warm
like a slug after a morning storm.

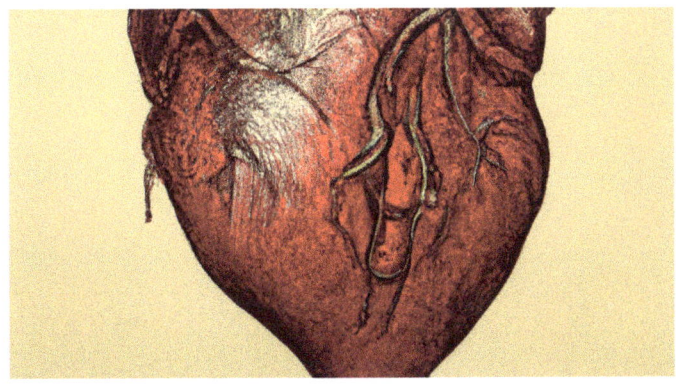

MY
STOMACH
DIVORCED
ME

Once I'm planted in a fresh
"La Taqueria" line,
Dolores rips herself clean,
makes for the   white marble exit

Can I still squash my craving?
The pinto beans greet me
in their bubbling pot.

At 20th & Mission, I clutch my desire.
I must, yes I must wolf down
a *lengua de res* burrito.

Two blocks south, Dolores gapes
at a mural's rabid-color heart.

When a beat cop
stumbles upon her, divorced
before the lavish

of Clarion Alley, does he know
        this organ belongs
to a rooted   San Francisco native?

In a ficus tree's hugging shade,
a beef tongue I named   Jesús
            slides down my throat.

He slaps onto concrete
and punches a rabid greyhound
tethered to a leash. Locals say

Jesús is on the lookout
            for a   *vaca*   missing its   *lengua*.

DOLORES PARK DRINKING

I chugged another Corona
in my Dolores Park circle of safety.

A San Francisco park crew
painted a starry sky of circles
on that spread of green

My friend Sophie said   *behavioral art*
back when we conquered

Tecates down Valencia glory
and before a Mission Street mural.

Within my circle, I was safe.
I took a long swig

despite Uncle Jerry
blabbing on I'll get Covid-19

from all these Coronas
I welcome into my body.
Empty bottle, I fell back into grass

with the California Golden Bear
roaring across my shirt's cotton front.

A text popped up: *Sophie is in the icu*
                      on a ventilator. Can you talk?

I shoved a new six-pack
into my liver's struggling arms.

MONDAY EXECUTiON

George ordered the hit on Sunday.
Once her body got left to the maggots
in The Cemetery of Executed Calendars,
Monday's ghost enrolled
at the Kansas Supernatural School.

She saw a prairie field glimmering
through a square of window
as she learned the arithmetic of revenge:
one assassin's buckshot
plus one buried workday
equals fire burning with a brain.

In his Olathe North High classroom
on Tuesday, George's lecture
on Washington's Crossing of the Delaware
plodded forward. After class,
he punished his neurons
with a plea: *is this the rest of my life?*

At Monday's sunrise graduation
that welcomed a Wednesday dawn,
she slipped her tornado-black gown
over her ghost frame
to ging a rhapsody ballad
on the valedictorian stage.

Olathe North's first period bell
vibrated. Students sat down
chattering like morning-birds.
George stood vacant under a wall clock.
Birds silent, he vomited the knowledge
he'd been regurgitating
down teenage ears
for a decade of solar resurrections.

Fire alarm pulled, he darted
one block home,
sand inside a scalding shower.
Steam and Blues rose
during his lathering

yet when he stepped
naked onto carpet, Monday dropped
a lit match. Stomping down stairs,
he halted before a dead-bolted door.

There he blinked from a window view
firefighter's storming through
North's brick entrance. Against fire
gaining consciousness, George screamed
with nobody left to listen.

51

I SCREWED MY BROTHER'S HEAD

on my Mom's body
because well
we needed a weekend party.

But now on the bee sting
of a Monday morning,

their corporate pronouns
are all tripped up.

When my Mom smudges drugstore
lipstick on my brother's lips,
he she they push

human-propelled sight
under tiled fluorescence

while whispers circle
from scavengers in suits.

IN REFLECTION, I SCREWED MY BROTHER'S HEAD

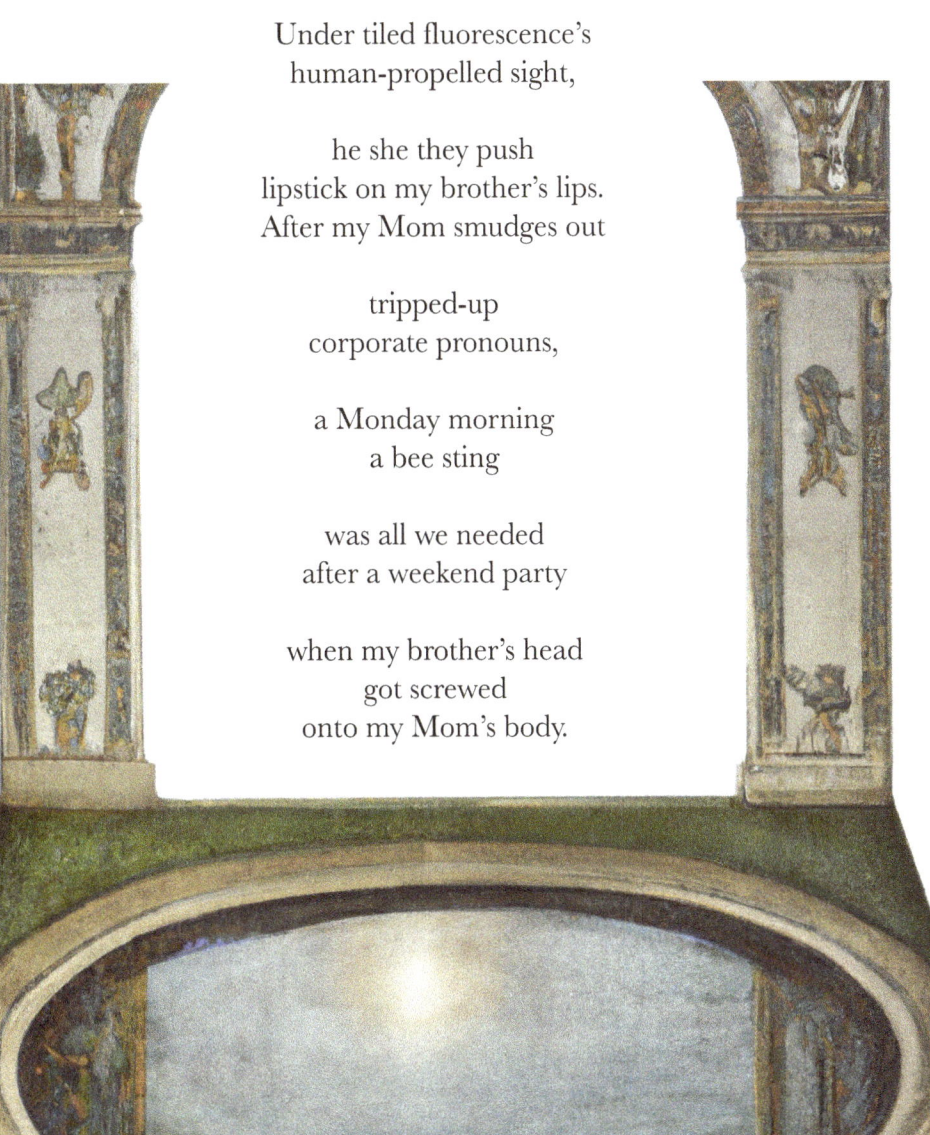

From scavengers in suits,
whispers circle.

Under tiled fluorescence's
human-propelled sight,

he she they push
lipstick on my brother's lips.
After my Mom smudges out

tripped-up
corporate pronouns,

a Monday morning
a bee sting

was all we needed
after a weekend party

when my brother's head
got screwed
onto my Mom's body.

On Monday, I sheathed out of my skin
in the parking lot.

My globule freckles
left rotting in the sun.

On Tuesday, I gave my liver
a brandy shower in the breakroom.

On Wednesday, I scooped out
my eyeballs, happy to display them

in a glass of ice tea
to my co-worker Cassandra.

On Thursday, I panfried
my testicles

for our spaghetti and meatballs
office party.

On Friday, I poked a pen
through my stomach lining

to write a Declaration of Protest
to the VP of Cadaver Development.

On hands and knees, I stuffed
my guts under his door

and walked out to my red car
past a slab of putrefied flesh.

A PRESCHOOL TEACHER'S GREETING

By the gurgling coffee maker,
Anna greeted Bryse
in the breakroom

after he lounged on a Sandwich,
Massachusetts beach.

When the retelling
of his seafood consumption
enlarged his words,

Anna naturally projected an image
of his stomach as an ocean:

the salmon and cod and lobster
he snapped, prodded, swallowed
into a transplanted haven

until a net snatched up a hot
lobster roll
and plopped it onto her plate.

AGE EDUCATION

My Mom educated me during our Mother's Day phone call: *you're 32 years old*. I believed her. I figured I forgot to switch my cognitive clock during my last birthday grooves.

So I slipped a note to a Union Square security guard: *I'm 32 years old. How old are you? Are you happy in your uniform?* I jumped onto a trolley car, which jolted away from the guard with white hair and a smile that charged like a buffalo across his face.

Before the Tenderloin's United Nations fountain, a man pushed a shopping cart with the sum of his life inside. I bought him a grass-grazed hamburger. His body needed a slab of cow. Trust me. A 32 year old has the body to know. Do you trust my body?

After I rode a 5 bus to Golden Gate Park, I screamed my age at a pile of black bison shit. The shit shrugged back *so what?*

Yet this morning over honey nut cheerios, I did the math: I'm really 31. Do you trust my math?

My Mom's laborious pushing first inflated my lungs 6 presidents ago. She's fastened to forget as a 63 — wait no — a 64-year-old woman. I called her. When her voicemail beeped, *I love you* stepped into my cell phone speaker like a hamburger consumed by a Tenderloin mouth.

FLAWED SKIN

I walked my white rose skin
 to Dr. Baskind

who smirked before she sliced
a petal from the bloom

of my body. Did they scream
when they got ripped from their native stem?

I know I am glorious.
I'm all that they knew

until Baskind dispatched them
to the lab. Did melanoma

poison my rose growth?
Test results pending.

DIET CRAZE

I skimmed a news headline
about some scientist finding sugar

in oxygen. So I'm cutting out oxygen
for a year. You mustn't worry
or drag your worry

to my Mom. I just want
to lose my pregnancy fat
before Dylan graduates

from preschool. She's learning
self care as I devour
chocolate bunnies

on Easter and Halloween
and every waxing moon.

At home, I hate telling her
the bunnies are my dinner.

Yes yes tomorrow
I'll be on day one
of showing my daughter

I have the control
to abstain from gulping down
what surrounds us.

NAKED

Locker room lights flicker
as I dry my body.

One bench over, a man
pulls up his boxers. We nod

then I flick my stare
back to the fabric
I will sheathe my body into.

I must ask: what if
this man swapped with you?

In our boyhoods
we splashed each other
in that Moraga bathtub.

Yet if we were naked now,
I would hide
in my locker, eat the key.

Here beside a stranger
under these dying bulbs,
I stand exposed.

Clothed on Webster Street,
I text you our Wednesday plan
in an evaporating winter day.

PIGEON SURVEY

I, the pigeon lord you bow before, flies low through the Tenderloin: a Sunset man disembarks a 38 bus and turns right onto Taylor Street. He moves with quick short strides.

When I survey this land of city government and feces, the man looks up and around but not too long into city eyes unless he wants to buy some crystal or powder. He doesn't want to buy an unknown high.

In the skin of a bloodline lord, I pierce his hippocampus: 3 rains ago, he walked through the Loin on Larkin Street. Before City Hall, he said *howa doing?* to a 20-something-year-old woman standing in a California buckeye's disjointed shadow. She stammered *hey hey now you you looking for something?* as she followed him to the next crossing signal.

The man steps into The Taylor Street Coffee Shop's Saturday stampede looping down the block. As he stands in a line of hungry bodies, a Tenderknob couple saunters back under assaulting sunlight. They each clutch a breakfast sando. After the wife takes a virgin bite, a bacon scrap falls. They move north towards affluence.

A royal in feathered attire, I swoop down to snatch discarded pig when the 20-something grabs that scrap off hot concrete.

65

III

YOU'VE LIVED
THIS STORY BEFORE

Instead of finding lucky pennies, you start finding lucky penises on sidewalks, floating in fountains, under couch cushions. In stores and restaurants, cashiers hand customers penises as currency. *Your change is two penises. Have a wonderful day.*

You throw your change against neighborhood concrete. Stomp on it. Rally the cells comprising your womanhood over masculine phallic penetrating your sight as you buy a *Ms. Magazine.* Flip inside,

a journalist catapults smooth language stones at the elected president — he wants you to believe a human only has dignity if they have a penis. Can you have dignity?

After your C-section, you asked the doctor why he cut your daughter out. He said *the vagina is a dirty place.*

Before the penis mint, your voice box of stone vibrates against workers leaving who will only start a new shift in a quick shaft of time. Once mosquitos encroach upon the gate's floodlight, your voice links into the Tuesday crowd chanting *Kick The Patriarchy Into The Past Tense!*

On Wednesday, your daughter's senior history teacher dictates: on your reward chart, *I will give you a penis sticker every day if you're on time, raise your hand, and don't talk back to me.*

She comes home and says *Mr. Jackson gave me my first sticker* as if her words came out stained.

With your grandfather clock's 4:00 o'clock chimes clanging in your ears, your husband flicks you away to claim the family's Thanksgiving turkey.

The dead bird you buy at checkout leaves you with one penis in your purse. The sales tax you must pay flings more penises into the body of our society.

You walk past a policeman on patrol. Down onto an ice-sleek sidewalk, he slaps you with his billy club penis. *Did you steal this turkey?* You show him your receipt — he tears it up. *You're a thief now.*

Behind retribution bars, you Curse and Sleep and Curse in your Sleep. When Curse is a protrusion on your tongue and Sleep claws at its face in the corner, you trace your C-section scar. Here no one invades your memory.

Your father bails you out. Back on driveway gravel, he joins your husband and brother to spit shame at you like Kansas hail punishing Earth.

At the kitchen table, your daughter wants to toss light onto your mind about the fourth-wave feminist novel she just read in secret. You slap her. She only gets louder. You cry.

You cry as you lock her bedroom door and turn away from banging on the inside. You don't want her to become a woman in a country you cannot love.

Men chatter what they anoint as gospel in the dining room. You sit still on a wooden chair until your husband demands you hand him the carving knife you cleaned. He stands in the stance of an American king triumphant over slaughtered meat. You smile as a lucky wife should.

NYC ART

From my window, I giggled
at a four-story-high
pink dick on a concrete wall.

The flower veins tickled my vision.
How could they not? I foresaw
the prudish pushing back
against that Alphabet
       City erection

but only my brother Aaron
and his castrated dog Mark
protested with pointed

signs and rhythmic chants
against hibiscus-pink
brushstrokes.

While Mark barked on Avenue C
under a red brick blaze,
I just gawked at Aaron

scampering up a ladder
with his roller rolling red paint
over this phallic proclamation.

With Sally purring at my feet,
I lit a smoke and stammered
> *does does Aaron believe*
> *art broke into a a home,*
> *vviolated a vvictim in their bed?*

On those days the L Train
won't stop rattling
my calm, I must search for
hibiscus in spring.

TONGUE SWAPPING I

Sally stole my poet tongue last night
while I dreamed
about an uprising of Whitman tongues.

When I awoke to a wound, she meowed
I already swapped yours
with Lenny the Lion.

After she sewed my ferocity in,
Sally led the way
to the Lafayette Street Bodega

where Simon greeted us
behind the domain of his counter.
Did you hear? We're selling
lion's milk now.

Once I groomed myself
with my sandpaper tongue,
I grabbed a quart
of interspecies delight.

South to Houston honking,
we sprinted down a F bus.
As I panted in this transit squeeze,
a businessman stepped

onto my wild identity
drooping across the black floor.
Naturally I growled

with an unfurled anger
into his cubicle eyes.
He cowered behind a blind woman

and I chugged back my quart
on that bus bumping over potholes to
The Central Park Zoo.

Ah yes, a new exhibit
spotlights Lenny the Lion.
We shamble up to his cage

to offer our milk
as he recites *Leaves of Grass*
from a diorama of fake nature.

STREET SALE

I price tag my memory
to pay my Oakland rent.

> *Five-Hundred Dollars*
> *For A Middle-Aged Hippocampus!*

> *A Personalized Tour Of My Boyhood*
> *For Another One-Hundred!*

I yell on a downtown corner
when Sally leaps down

from an oak tree. With her claws
extended, she hisses

> *no one is gonna buy*
> *your moldy memory.*

Out of the crowd,
a woman who makes

my brain smile
steps into my shadow.

> *I am in your memory.*
> *Why are you selling me off?*

MUTANT

The radioactive ████████████████ waste
               my home   sleeps on
    seeped into   Sarah's brain
                   ████████████████

           as she twisted our sheets
into a knot   ████████ neurological reject
At dawn   her eyes   snapped ████████████ open
like a turtle   in attack

When we   raided ████████████████
the pancake table   ████████████ the syrup   ████████
           sloshed in her   mouth████

morphed into   a puddle of oil ████████
from her engine-   gurgling   stomach

Was my girlfriend   a product
    of cellular   ████████████████ driven combustion

With the clouds   unzipping   a downtown rattle

I punch through ████████████ a nexus of hail
      stinging my *Homo sapient*   skull ████

MUTANT
REDACTED

▮ Radioactive ▮▮▮▮ waste

seeped into   Sarah's brain

                as she twisted ▮▮▮▮

▮ a ▮▮▮▮▮▮▮▮▮▮▮▮ neuroloigical reject

At dawn   her eyes   ▮▮▮▮▮▮▮▮▮▮
▮▮▮▮▮▮   in attack

W▮▮e   raided ▮▮▮▮▮▮
▮▮▮▮▮▮▮▮▮▮▮▮▮
▮▮▮▮▮▮▮▮▮▮▮▮▮

▮▮▮▮▮▮ a puddle of oil ▮▮▮▮▮▮▮
from her engine-   gurgling   stomach

Was my girlfriend   ▮▮▮▮
▮▮▮▮cellular ▮▮▮▮▮▮   driven combustion

WIth the clouds   unzipping   a ▮▮▮▮rattle

I punch ▮▮▮▮▮▮▮ a nexus of hail
        stinging my   ▮▮▮▮   skull ▮▮▮▮

TONGUE SWAPPING 2

I swallowed my tongue
on white bedroom carpet,
shat it out, swapped it
with my neighbor Elizabeth.

Now Elizabeth swoons my girlfriend
Sarah in my voice. Sarah
is down yet peppers out questions:

Does this make me gay?
Can you wear our dildo tonight?
Do you have any lube?

she barks over her black IPA
at a highway bar. They swerve home
past my red robin door.

Transpose through, I rattle
Elizabeth's tongue before her husband.
Elizabeth and William made theirs
official in Las Vegas.

Under lamplight, is this a roadside love?
I search William's suburban eyes
for a future I'll grasp

in our nursing home days.
when I speak in our present groove,
he silences me with a wet kiss.

81

REBELLIOUS
TESTICLES

Mary and Barry climaxed
a constitution
onto the burgundy curtain
that draped the window
David once shared with Sarah.

On-a-hit-your-head-kinda-morning,
he smothered the semen
of their freedom lines.

After Barry breathed deep into a paper sack
and Mary prayed to her deity,
David welcomed them back
to proudly balloon
as his testosterone Gods of manhood.

At dusk, he masticated
a bowl of lobster ravioli.
All seemed well
until some marinara
coalesced on his chin.

During a tongue stretching
to lick that red away,
those balls wrenched themselves free.

They rolled along
the cul-de-sac's curved spine
through a foreign front door
into the screams
of Sarah's dildo climax.

In that bedroom, Barry and Mary
remembered their orgasmic offerings
once splayed before the burgundy
David now burns in a ball-less night.

SLEEPING WITH
THE MOON

When I dated Neil Armstrong back in the 70's he insisted on
sleeping with his stolen moon rock
He stuffed this four-billion-year-old friend
under his pillow as he dreamed one July night
of kicking up 1969 dust   dust that clung to his spacesuit.
Ohio-born heartbeats encased within

His dream disassembled on a pillow   caught in morning light
Over buttered toast   I confessed a watermelon need
pressing on my mind
We strode through   a roadside farmer's market
after Neil dropped his rock into his breast pocket
I glowed in his warmth

until a horde of tomato lovers clamored to his celebrity
To tranquil my bones   I breathed deep
like my mother taught me
Once he bought my need with the fame of his face
honey please, you wouldn't charge Neil Armstrong
I imagined stealing his stolen rock   and throwing it into passing traffic
A windshield splintered
as I pulled my back tight beside a man no longer king

Instead   I watched him slice into that green globe
With exposed red   flaunting our eyes   I snatched a slice
and walked home alone
with black ocean seeds sliding down my throat under the sun rising
in a cut-open shine

84

PABLO'S FRIEND

On BART in West Oakland,
a Lyft driver Pablo knows
steps aboard with her teenager in tow.
Their conversation spins
like a film reel under the Bay.

Last December, Pablo ordered
a car to Zachary's Pizza
beneath clouds joining hands
into thunderclap.

When Bethany found him soaked,
he squished onto the passenger seat
while she drove north up Shattuck.

Once he said *I'm a preschool teacher,*
she stared back with loud eyes.
> *After 3 kids and 3 abortions,*
> *I got my tubes tied at 30.*

Pablo grins at the mother-and-daughter combo
aboard this inbound train.
They jostle into a downtown stop
where he's meant to disembark
but his feet fail to move.

> *Are you happy, Bethany?*
The doors slide shut
without a fight. She beams.
> *I'm working on it. Are you?*

CITY BRAIN

I leaned my neural ganglia
of dirt road   origin
up against The Millennium Tower
Pa welded a decade ago
when sparks leapt   like rabid rabbits

I've come to a cold San Francisco slap
where air swirls in   steel   canyons
but I will not grow a city brain
in some urban garden
when the lettuce heads
back home are screaming   my name

IN THE SKIN
OF A PIG

In his MIle High seat, John
drank a dollar for every ounce
that guzzled past his Bronco-loving voice box

At halftime, John squeezed
onto a bathroom line's
shifting tongue

into a tiled room
where a long metal trough
dragged his brain

back to his boyhood's
family farm: pigs
crowded into a common knot
around the slop at feeding time

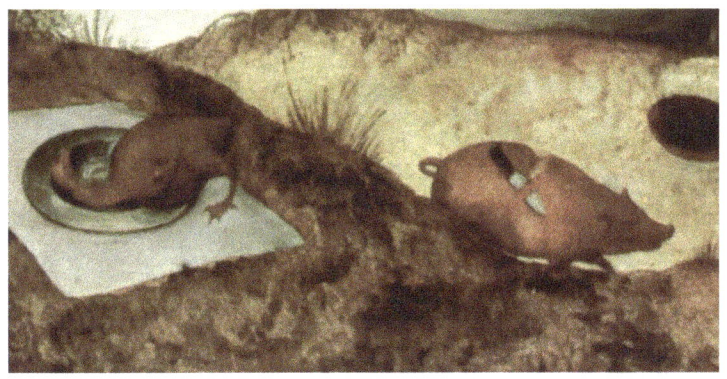

like fans lining up side by side,
one drain welcoming
every man's piss.

John walked to an open slot
but with the line behind
and dicks all around,
his water balloon couldn't be popped.

Zip up, he shuffled his shy bladder
back to seat 7C
of testosterone worship.

WOMAN-CAT TIME

Mary sank a stare
into her new boyfriend

when she walked out of his apartment
with Saly meowing *let's go*

He got left alone
sucking on iced coffee.
Satisfaction brewed

where Sally strutted her paws
and Mary's boots thumped
through mid-day rain

into the beckoning mouth
of Broadway Street.

Once he texted her an angry
face emoji, Mary hissed back

the necessity of Woman-Cat Time
without a man throwing his voice
onto that wet concrete tongue.

A BODY PARTS COMEDY

Do you remember ten springs ago? Back in that season of renewal, I remember gulping down IPAs at a now-closed dive bar with my roommates. At Market & Fremont, we wobbled onto the crosswalk in a pack of testosterone as a klatch of estrogen strode toward us.

Under this intersection's red light, a woman offered me $20 for my corduroy pants. Would you plunge this transaction forward? I stripped down in San Francisco headlight glare gawking at my melanin whiteness.

My brain can't wrestle down the truth though I'm certain I used my newfound money for a special dinner of either Rocky Mountain oysters or dos tacos de lengua.

I still have my tongue so I'll slingshot you this story I've hashed out

pantless with tacos or testicles digesting inside. You decide. Did I stop there? I danced on the plague marking the division between landfill and bedrock, between sleepwalking and an awakened state.

Before a hotel window painted with vomit, I hugged the doorwoman as if she was my mother. I remember a memory I never had when I suckled milk from her breast. Down the block, a drum- and-guitar band played "Like a Rolling Stone" for BART riders to toss in change.

Under a bus stop shelter, I found security beside a man waiting for a 38 bus. With a smoke resting on his lips, he bought my Psycho T-shirt for $10.

Pantless and shirtless over at 6th & Powell, a black high heel sliced my own heel. Flat on my ass, I gaped up at a woman shrieking what can I do? Well she bought my boxer briefs for $25. When she rang her boyfriend, Donovan came right over. I sold him my dick for $50 — he now sports two dicks.

Naked in weekend shadow, I shook their hands with blood smeared on my palm.

Under the Tenderloin Museum awning, my skin, sinew, and muscle went for a penny to a soul shivering under their thin blanket. I clutched the sum of my body's value as I rushed past without staring at a homeless vet sleeping in his wheelchair at Everywhere & Taylor. Clank clanking on shit-stained concrete,

I snaked up into Nob Hill where I finally found my heaven after an employee removed an old mannequin from a storefront display. The owner hired me without even an interview.

How glorious! Swing by soon — I feel alive whenever a customer nods in approval and purchases the business casual attire my skeleton frame advertises.

Hired hands undress me every night. In the morning, I'm propped back up with a clean suit gleaming in affluent sunlight.

A BODY █████ COMEDY

Do you remember █████████████████ that season of
renewal, I remember gulping down IPAs at █████████
█████████████████████████ Market & Fremont, we
wobbled onto the crosswalk in a pack████████████ as a
klatch ██████████ strode toward us

███████████████████████████ where a woman offered
me $20 for my corduroy pants. Would you plunge ███
██████████ forward█ into stripping down in San Francisco
headlight glare? ██████████████████████████

██
██
████████████████████████████████

████████████████████I'll slingshot you this story I've
hashed out

pantless with tacos or testicles digesting inside. You decide.
Did I stop there? I danced █████████████████████
██
█████████████████████

before a hotel window painted with vomit, I hugged the
doorwoman as if she was my mother. I remember a
memory I never had when I suckled milk from her breast.

██
████████████████████████████████

Under a bus stop shelter, I found ████████ a man waiting for ██████████ a smoke to rest ███ on his lips, he bought my ██████ T-shirt ██████.

Pantless and shirtless ████████████████, a black high heel sliced my ████████████ my ass, I gaped up at a woman shrieking. ██████████████ Well she bought my boxer briefs for $25. ██████ She ████████████████████████████████ ██████████████████████████ now sports two dicks.

Naked in weekend shadow, I shook ██████████████ blood smeared on my palm.

Under the Tenderloin Museum awning, my ████ sinew ███ ██████ went for a penny to a soul shivering under their thin blanket. I clutched the sum of my body's value as I ████████ ███████████████████████████████████████ ████████████████████ clank clanked on shit-stained concrete▌

██████████ into Nob Hill where ████████████████████ ████ an employee removed an old mannequin from a storefront display. The owner hired me ████████████████████.

How ████████████████████████ alive I feel whenever a customer nods ██████████ and purchases the ████████████ attire my skeleton ██████ advertises.

Hired hands undress me ████████████████████████████ I'm propped back up ████████████ gleaming in ██████████ sunlight.

IV

THE GHOST CHILD

In New Year rain, Matthew's red car
skidded into a   child
who walked with his mother
across   a   crosswalk.

In her kitchen domain, Mary wrote an elegy
for the linked hemispheres of her mind
beneath a pot roast recipe.

Matthew stepped inside
to her cookbook thudding shut.
She smiled flaccid,   pulled a carcass   from the oven.
After they swallowed chunks of succulence,

they commanded themselves to sleep.
With their bodies in temporary   death,
the ghost child

possessed a   doll
Mary propped on a shelf
for their unborn   daughter.

They awoke to the fallen doll
wailing on washed hardwood.

                            By Matthew's command,
            Mary burned it
          over a stovetop flame.

At dawn, sunrise rays   couldn't survive
                   San Francisco   clouds.
Mary brewed his coffee,
bandaged the burns

she inflicted.   By Matthew's command,
she carried the doll to Pioneer Park
where her elegy limped off her tongue

until enough soil
smothered that ghost   face.

HUMANOID

You're ready to build a daughter.
First, plop in a pig's heart
into a baby skeleton

six months old. The vessel jerks
alive while you wipe away blood
streaked across your forehead.

Breathe. Now stuff
goat lungs up her chest

and superglue the knees
of a brown bear onto her sockets.

Since this product
requires a brain, you hustle in
a neurological universe:

the capacity of a calf
cries within a scoop of sunlight
as you bend over to soothe and staple gun

pig skin down over familial anatomy.
Your six-month-old daughter died;

you carry her humanoid self
across your buffalo grass backyard.

Tell her your Grandma's parable.
Raise her as your own.

NAKED IN THE
WAITING ROOM

I get there eight minutes early —
try to find Tuesday comfort
alongside my fellow neurotics

when my physician, Dr. Samson,
checks-in at the front desk
to join our patient company.

We offer nods through stiff air
as she sits on a black uniform cushion,
one in a cluster of dissimilar pain.

Should I greet her? High-five? Banter
about her baby and the quality
of undressing emotions
to the same licensed mind?

Dr. Samson grabs a magazine,
throws her sight down.
I sit like an exposed nerve.

I must prepare to verbalize
how a husbandhood — no — a manhood
flaw moves with ease within me.

My therapist stands in the doorway.
He holds a file
that encloses my flaw. His voice
a beacon I follow

by streaming past Dr. Samson
who's just Emily now.
I have an appointment with her
slotted for tomorrow.

Will she find a fatherhood-strong
sperm count? I'll talk about it
next Tuesday at 3:00 o'clock.

SWIVEL TALK

I sit within the sterile walls
of Dr. Samson's office
where she implores

you can still be a father

even when my right testicle
holds hollow bullets.

My father had the same condition
you have. I'm here today.

I can't deny her synaptic existence
as her swivel chair squeaks.

At home under our bedroom glare,
I smile over my left testicle's
sperm ammunition

and pat the other like a hairy dog
in need of love

when you strut in
with only your bra and panties on.

I'm ovulating. Are you ready?
Are you ready? I ask my army.

They nod their militaristic body   yes.

FATHERHOOD
IN SHADOW

Last night I dreamed
my shadow fucked Mary's shadow:
our shadow baby

unlocked the front door
and sucked his thumb
under the neighbor's lemon tree.

Once I discovered his escape
in enveloping shade,
I plucked a yellow globe,

sliced it in two, squeezed juice
into his expanding eyes.
A father must first teach his kin
pain is born with a heartbeat

that sprinted alongside
my shadow joy and I
in a Golden Gate exodus.
Through descending fog,

I grabbed the lemon's other half,
burned holes into red metal.
Acid sizzled

when my mind shakes awake.
I jolt out of bed, push against
a Telegraph Hill wind.

After I assault my heart up that concrete insult
beside the command of a Coit Tower skyline,
I buy an orange balloon at a tourist store.

Within sight of a ferry bound for Alcatraz,
I find my wife waiting in Dr. Samson's office.
I offer Mary my balloon, she offers me
a sperm cup. We'll soon know my worth.

WHEN A POLLUTED RAINBOW

skinned his violet knee
on park asphalt, you sprinted towards
smoke-inhaled colors
bleeding into your cupped hands.

Past a knot of trees
that once squawked
on diseased branches,
your paternal grip
carried his body home.

Under a spiked kitchen light,
you cradled Roy G. Biv
until he cried out
the industrial smoke
no longer infecting
our orphaned son.

BIG SKY KIN

I hug 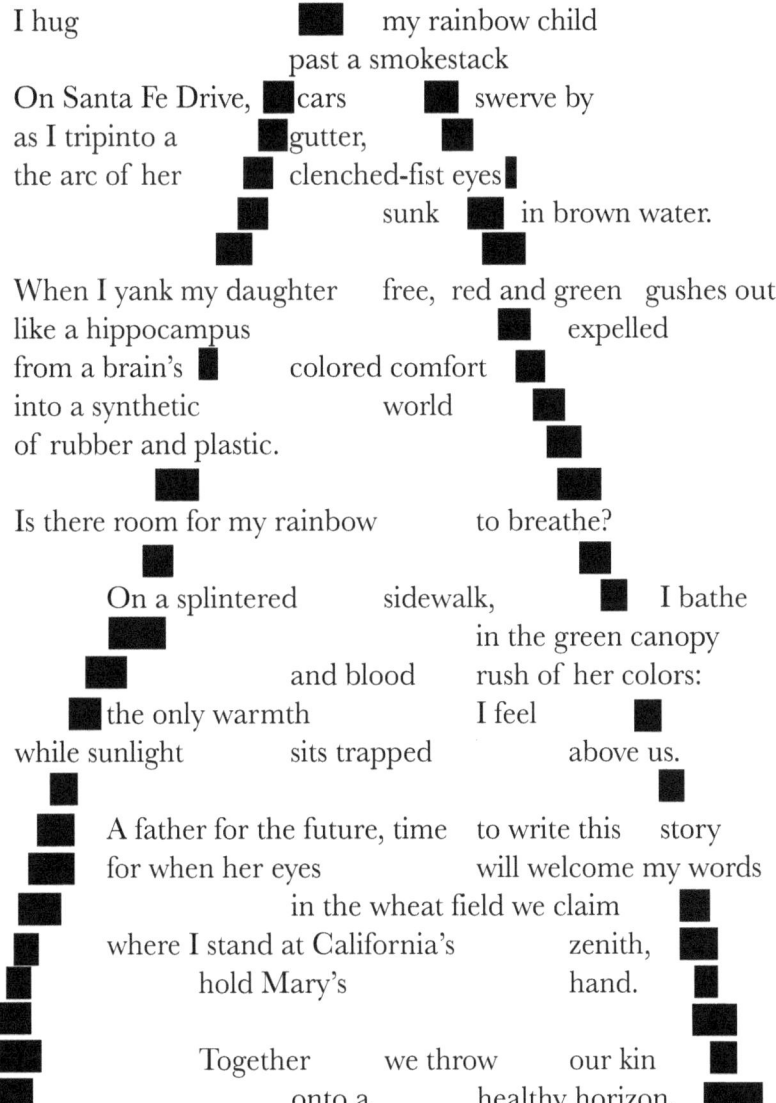 my rainbow child
past a smokestack
On Santa Fe Drive, cars swerve by
as I tripinto a gutter,
the arc of her clenched-fist eyes
sunk in brown water.

When I yank my daughter free, red and green gushes out
like a hippocampus expelled
from a brain's colored comfort
into a synthetic world
of rubber and plastic.

Is there room for my rainbow to breathe?

On a splintered sidewalk, I bathe
in the green canopy
and blood rush of her colors:
the only warmth I feel
while sunlight sits trapped above us.

A father for the future, time to write this story
for when her eyes will welcome my words
in the wheat field we claim
where I stand at California's zenith,
hold Mary's hand.

Together we throw our kin
onto a healthy horizon.

111

KIN REDACTED

After our rainbow child
coughs past
a smokestsack

she trips
into a gutter
Her fisted eyes
sink into American water

Once I expel her
from backwater confinement

green and red
gushes free
from her brain's
colored comfort

into a world
of burning rainbows

A father for the future
time to write this story
of when I drag
her flame thrashed body

to the wheat field we claim
where I hold your hand

Together we stand
over our kin
before a smoky horizon

113

FAMILY REUNION

When my in-laws
stomped into my scrubbed home,

I took a rag to their torsos,
noses, inner thighs

where dirt signed a lease
to live on skin I married into.

Around my dining room table,
two bodies still screamed

rancid as they ripped
their brown teeth

through my blackened
chicken legs.

Next they gulped down
my red wine, sloshing
into their sloppy mouths.

As I washed the dishes
in a froth of soap,

elongated tongues
licked stemmed glasses

like snakes smelling
family air.

BABY OR VACATION

Mary and I argued
and then fucked.
Or did we fuck first and argue later?

Wine blurs time yet I know
we spat back and forth

about whether to have a baby
or take a vacation

since both throw
kitchens of carbon
into Earth's buckling atmosphere.

Well once Mary picked a trip
to make our matrimony complete,

we left our heated
apartment empty
to fly overnight through warming air.

On seats later dropped into beds, we got served
two hamburgers, which required

twenty-six-thousand gallons of water
and hectares of deforested farmland
to graze and slaughter cows.

After check-in, we screamed out the recipe
for a vacation baby
over that stained mattress spread.

The oven of Mary's body
now bakes a zygote

like the grocery bags
we will fill with meat
to feed our future kin.

MAMA UNIVERSE

Remember when we stumbled   through that hotel door
          with beef and wine   sloshing around   inside
You buckled before   the burgundy curtain pulsating color
          when my gravity-strength moved upon you

Look at our baby   She floats   while perpetually attached
          like a spacewalking astronaut tethered to steel
to your uterine wall   at the junction of nutritional flow

          Under Sunday's strawberry moon
     I bend an ear down   to your belly
          listen to a heliocentric heartbeat
          learning to gravitationally grasp life

Can your solar tongue shine   over the verses
               of Bishop and Dickinson and Brooks
I want her to know   she will have a voice in this   America

     Ultrasound pixels display our baby galaxy's growth
     within the sweep of a Mama   Universe you call
                                        my body

EAST BAY SEED

When the rat climbing up the wall
makes a seedy flower go bloom, my organs
rearrange themselves in frightful frenzy.
Rat fur does that to my nervous system.

It's strange mouse fur
doesn't coax the same response
from the bundle of neurons

coiled up like a garden hose
in the backyard of the Berkeley home
I'm priced-out of ever owning.

In this $50-a-night space, I sprawl across a bed
I've resigned myself to sleep
on the bodily fluids spilled before me.
They haunt like a nefarious realtor.

As the rat and I breathe the same air, can a rat
buy a financial smile? I know seediness
scurries beyond one motel room's interior
into the city cage that encloses

a California living room
Mary and I have yet to plant our feet in
with a For Sale sign
skewered into grass out front.

SEED

I am a seed ███████ in you.
Will you water the soil
enveloping my growth?

Watch. I burst within
a Mother I already love
even without ██████████my brain's

nectar smile
that will pollinate

my heart of red petals
in a dawn waiting to be ███ born.

ON DISPLAY

We sit in suburban radiation
while neighbors swarm
around your baby heart
building arteries within you.

Steve and Ellen push in.
After they hear of the steam shower
I installed, they implore
you wash myself anew
the first chance you get.

You nod, excuse your mind away.
Where did you go? I know
the home we insured

shouts *I Do* across our fertilized lawn.
Soon our daughter's feet will find
escape on sweeping grass.

When salad dressing spills
on your blue petal dress, your mother
commands you find a new flower to wear
but you pluck her voice away,
wear your stain planted into design cloth.

You crush ice between your molars.
I know you want to scream.
Instead, your tongue is a clipped bird.

I kiss your cheek, whisper
this will all be over soon.
Ellen's camera clicks to capture this.

At last, presents get stacked
like a downtown crowding the table.
Time to flee behind sunglasses
against a gathering of eyes
who only see our smiles on display.

BEGINNINGS

Let's travel back   Are you ready
                    Yes   remember our first fluid
        Our marriage selves never met   our fetal selves
when we existed   without the verbal mud we throw
        over raising a resilient pit bull   or   child

            I come home to Sam barking   hello
                                by the kitchen island
as your body   builds a femur   on the loveseat
Through the window
                            a honeysuckle sapling vaults
                    toward our common   sky

BIRTH

/ You got taught your womb is a baby
factory / your hair an assembly line of
beauty / your body a bacteria gauntlet / you
gifted me when I came out gasping / yet our
skinned skeleton(s) surpasses any factory

        thumbprint / while we breathe within ficus
        shade / I stand before a XX biomass / I'm
        pledging all my cells to / like the delivery
        microorganisms / you secreted onto my pink
        self /

Birthing a Beginning

I heard you got taught
your womb is an assembly line
of beauty. Your *I Do* self

never met your first fluid self.
Within a skin shell, you existed

before you got taught
your womb is a baby factory.
Did I say beauty
back at the beginning?

Take out my heart, throw
verbal mud
across the kitchen island

when I come home to Sam barking
as your body builds a brain.

I stand before you, a XX biomass
I'm pledging all my microorganisms to.

Out back, a ficus sapling springs
toward our common blue.

Through the window
our skinned skeletons surpasses
any factory thumbprint

when our marriage selves
travel
to the loveseat

The loveseat says
hello

Birthing a Be

I heard you got taught
your womb is an assembly line
of beauty. Your *I Do* self

Through the window
our skinned ...etons surpasses
any factory
...t

bef...
y... never met your first fluid self, you existed
Within a skin shell, you existed
...aught
Did ... say beauty ...o is a baby factory.
back at the be...
...ning?
Take out my heart, thro
verbal mud
across the kitchen island

when our marriage selves
travel
to the loveseat

when I come home to Sam barking
as your body builds a brain.

The loveseat says
hello

Out ...
I stand before you, a XX biomass
I'm pledging all my microorganisms to
...pling springs
...mmon blue.

131

NOTES

Illustrations

Cover: Detail from Hieronymus Bosch, *The Garden of Earthly Delights*. Museo del Prado, Madrid. Design by Audrey Mei

I Woke Up: "A renaissance style drawing of mangrove roots with a light parchment background," generated by OpenAI.

Stone Baby: Detail from Hieronymus Bosch copyist, *Adoration of the Chrsit Child*, c. 1568. Rijksmuseum Amsterdam, Amsterdam.

Hibiscus in Our Bedroom: "A renaissance style drawing of a red hibiscus with filaments on a parchment background," generated by OpenAI.

Log Parabel: Detail Detail from Hieronymus Bosch, *The Garden of Earthly Delights: The Hell*. Museo del Prado, Madrid.

Heartless: Map, Siege of 's-Hertogenbosch, 1613-1615.

Animal Switch: Hierynomus Bosch follower, *The Last Judgement*, c. 1506-1508. Alte Pinakothek, Munich.

I Left My North Oakland Shadow: "Dramatic drawing of a red human heart in Lenardo Da Vinci style," generated by OpenAI

My Stomach Divorced Me: Detail from Hieronymus Bosch, *The Garden of Earthly Delights*. Museo del Prado, Madrid.

Monday Execution: Generated by OpenAI

In Reflection, I Screwed My Brother's Head: "medieval painting of a reflecting pool, white background," generated by OpenAI

Workweek: Detail from Hieronymus Bosch, *The Conjurer*. Musée Municipal, Saint-Germain-en-Laye.

Flawed Skin: Detail from Hieronymus Bosch, *The Garden of Earthly Delights*. Museo del Prado, Madrid.

Naked: Detail from Hieronymus Bosch, *The Garden of Earthly Delights*. Museo del Prado, Madrid.

Pigeon Survey: "Medieval painting of a powerfaul flying pigeon, frontal view," generated by OpenAI

NYC Art: Detail from Hieronymus Bosch, *The Garden of Earthly Delights*. Museo del Prado, Madrid.

Tongue Swapping: Right, detail from Hieronymus Bosch, *The Garden of Earthly Delights*. Museo del Prado, Madrid. Left: detail from Hieronymus Bosch, *The Adoration of the Magi*, 1485-1500. Museo del Prado, Madrid.

Sleeping with the Moon: Hieronymus Bosch, *Ascent of the Blessed*. 1505-1515. Gallerie dell'Accademia, Venice.

City Brain: Detail from Hieronymus Bosch, *The Last Judgment*, c. 1486. Groeningemuseum, Bruges.

In the Skin of a Pig: Detail from Pieter Bruegel the Elder, *Land of Cockaigne*, 1567. Alte Pinakothek, Munich.

Woman-Cat Time: Detail from unknown artist, *Scheibler'sches Wappenbuch , älterer Teil. Shield of the Laiming Family*, 1450-580. Bayerische Staatsbibliothek Cod.icon. 312. Munich.

The Ghost Child: Detail from Hieronymus Bosch, *Child with Pinwheel and Toddler's Chair*, c. 1500. Kunsthistorisches Museum, Vienna.

Swivel Talk: Detail from Hieronymus Bosch, *Triptych of the Temptation of St. Anthony*, c. 1501. Museu Nacional de Arte Antiga, Lisbon.

Fatherhood in Shadow: Detail from Hieronymus Bosch, *The Garden of Earthly Delights*. Museo del Prado, Madrid.

Mama Universe: Hieronymus Bosch, *Creation*, external shutters of *The Garden of Earthly Delights*. Museo del Prado, Madrid.

Seed: Detail from Hieronymus Bosch, *The Garden of Earthly Delights*. Museo del Prado, Madrid.

ACKNOWLEDGEMENTS

Grateful acknowledgements are made to the following journals in which these poems (in some cases, earlier versions) originally appeared or are forthcoming:

3 Moon Literary Magazine: "The Radioactive Horse"

Alt Beast Zine: "Rubber Magic" (Retitle)

Bending Genres Journal: "A Body Parts Comedy"

Colossus:Home: "East Bay Seed"

Down in the Dirt Magazine: "Naked"

Eclectica Magazine: "A Preschool Teacher's Greeting" (Retitle)

Five 2 One Magazine: "Runaway Legs"

Fredericksburg Literary Art and Review: "Confession"

Garfield Lake Review: "I Screwed My Brother's Head" and "Diet Craze"

Levitate Literary Magazine: "Baby or Vacation"

Likely Red: "I Woke Up"

Muurje Project: "Runaway Legs" (Reprint)

New Millennium Writings (Monthly Muse #4 Award Winner): "Beginnings"

Orange Quarterly (2017 Green House Poetry Prize Finalist): "City Brain"

Poetry Festival: "Fatherhood in Shadow" (Retitle)

Someone Tell Us Where We're Going: Poets Wanted Anthology 2020: "Based on a True Story," "I Left My North Oakland Shadow," "Tongue Swapping 1," and "Tongue Swapping 2"

Sooth Swarm Journal: "Age Education"

sPARKLE & blink: "Workweek" and "Humanoid"

Speculative City: "Mutant"

Typewriter Emergencies: "Animal Switch"

Who Do You Think You Are? (Podcast: "Is This A Practical Talk Or A Spiritual Talk?"): "Hibiscus in the Bedroom"

Witches 'n Pink: "You're Guilty of Being a Woman" (Retitle) and "The Ghost Child" (Retitle)

Keith Gaboury earned his MFA in Creative Writing from Emerson College. His poems have appeared in such literary publications as *Poetry Quarterly, New Millennium Writings*, and the San Francisco Public Library's Poem of the Day Series. Kelsay Books published *The Cosmos is Alive* in 2023. He's a preschool teacher, a proud bibliophile, and the president of the Berkeley Branch of the California Writers Club. Keith lives in Oakland, California.

Learn more at keithgaboury.com.